KITTENS

KITTENS

An Illustrated Treasury

Compiled by Michelle Lovric

COURAGE BOOKS

an imprint of
RUNNING PRESS
Philadelphia, Pennsylvania

Cover design by Toby Schmidt
Cover illustration by Henriette Ronner
Interior design by Lili Schwartz
Edited by Melissa Stein
Typography by Deborah Lugar

Published by Courage Books, an imprint of Running Press Book Publishers
125 South Twenty-second Street
Philadelphia, Pennsylvania 19103–4399

The author gratefully acknowledges the permission of the following to reproduce copyrighted material in this book:

P. 12 and p. 27: From *Particularly Cats and More Cats* by Doris Lessing, first published in Great Britain by Michael Joseph in 1967. Copyright © 1967 Doris Lessing. Reprinted by permission of Jonathan Clowes Ltd., London, on behalf of Doris Lessing.

P. 13: From *Down the Garden Path* by Beverley Nichols, first published in Great Britain by Jonathan Cape in 1932 and reprinted in 1983 by The Antique Collectors' Club. Copyright © 1983 Beverley Nichols. Permission courtesy of Eric Glass Ltd.

P. 15 and p. 45: From "Blue Persian" and "Phoenix" from *Cat Poems* by Jacintha Buddicom, published by Leslie Frewin Publishers Ltd. in Great Britain. Copyright © 1973 Jacintha Buddicom. Permission courtesy of the author.

P. 18: From *Intimate Things* by Karel Čapek, published by George Allen and Unwin, now Unwin Hyman, an imprint of HarperCollins Publishers Ltd. Copyright © 1935 Karel Čapek.

P. 20: Quotation from *A Passion for Cats*, edited by Philip Wood, first published in Great Britain by David & Charles. Copyright © 1987 Cats Protection League.

P. 28 and 33: From *Supercat* by Grace McHattie, first published in Great Britain by Methuen, London. Copyright © Grace McHattie.

P. 30: From *The Silent Miaow: A Manual for Kittens, Strays and Homeless Cats, Translated from the Feline and Edited by Paul Gallico, with Picture Story by Suzanne Szasz*, first published in the United States by Crown Publishers, Inc., New York, and in Great Britain by Souvenir Press. Copyright © 1964 Paul Gallico and Suzanne Szasz and copyright © 1964 Mathemata A.G.

P. 35: From *Stray* by A. N. Wilson, first published in Great Britain by Walker Books Ltd. and in the United States by Orchard Books. Copyright © 1987 A. N. Wilson.

P. 39: From *Kubus, My Friend the Cat*, by Czeslaw Bednarczyk, translated by Margaret Watson, first published in Great Britain by Poets and Painters Press in 1988. Copyright © 1988 Czeslaw Bednarczyk.

P. 42: From "The Silent Purr" by Stephanie Wilson from *Catatonic 2*, edited by Don Turner, first published in Great Britain by Ghost Publishing in aid of the Cats Protection League. Copyright © 1994 Stephanie Wilson.

P. 47: From *The Walled Garden* by Michael Bullock, first published in Canada by Ekstasis Editions. Copyright © 1992 Michael Bullock.

INTRODUCTION

Kittens are a triumph of choreography, combining the grace of ballet with the slapstick timing of farce. Unguarded in its expressions, a kitten personifies astonishment, embarrassment, and fear with a candor that a grown cat soon learns to disdain. As we watch a small fierce kitten stalk and pounce, we may glimpse the elegant cat to come.

For a short, precious time, we delight in the continuous spectacle of a kitten's innocent playfulness. But in the midst of its winsome capers, sprightly and roguish, a kitten can fix us with the intense unblinking stare of a grownup cat, a look that embodies the mystery of the species. After all, part of the charm of kittenhood is that it is fleeting.

Gathered here are words and images in celebration of the kitten, capturing the irresistible appeal of these mischievous creatures.

A kitten is in the animal world
what a rosebud is in a garden.

ROBERT SOUTHEY (1774–1843)
ENGLISH WRITER

Kittenhood, the baby time. . . . of cats,

is with most the brightest, sprightliest,

and prettiest period of their existence,

and perhaps the most happy.

Harrison Weir (1824–1906)
English artist and writer

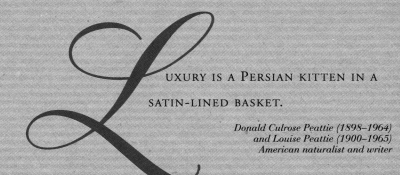

*L*UXURY IS A PERSIAN KITTEN IN A
SATIN-LINED BASKET.

Donald Culrose Peattie (1898–1964)
and Louise Peattie (1900–1965)
American naturalist and writer

. . . the daintiest little kitten imaginable. It was just like a swan's down powder-puff.

THEOPHILE GAUTIER (1811–1872)
FRENCH POET AND WRITER

When my eyes wander from cat
Who so intoxicates me with love
And my eyes slowly return to me
Gazing back within my mind,

I see to my surprise
The fire of his pale iris,
Bright ember, swirling pearl,
Hypnotising me with his
        fixed eyes. . . .

Ultra-pink peony . . .
Silver Siamese soft cat . . .
Gold-dust butterfly. . . .

BUSON (1716–1783)
JAPANESE POET AND PAINTER

THE KITTEN WAS SIX WEEKS OLD. IT WAS ENCHANTING, A DELICATE FAIRY-TALE CAT. . . . FROM THE FRONT, SITTING WITH HER SLENDER PAWS STRAIGHT, SHE WAS AN EXOTICALLY BEAUTIFUL BEAST. SHE SAT, A TINY THING, IN THE MIDDLE OF A YELLOW CARPET, SURROUNDED BY FIVE WORSHIPPERS, NOT AT ALL AFRAID OF US. THEN SHE STALKED AROUND THAT FLOOR OF THE HOUSE, INSPECTING EVERY INCH OF IT, CLIMBED UP ON TO MY BED, CREPT UNDER THE FOLD OF A SHEET, AND WAS AT HOME.

Doris Lessing, b. 1919
Persian-born English writer

Cats simply ought not to be allowed to go about, radiating such distracting charm.

BEVERLEY NICHOLS (1898–1983)
ENGLISH WRITER

You flirt with me as a concubine in
robes of silk.

AMY LOWELL (1874–1925)
AMERICAN WRITER

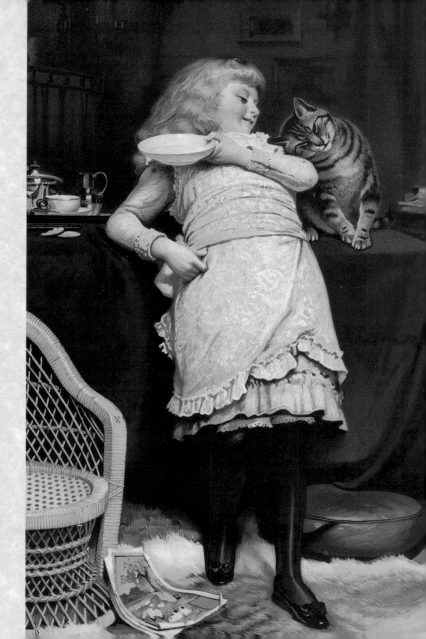

Long dark grey fur

And Egypt in your eyes,

Your Nile-green eyes, my kitten

Cleopatra:

What Lion-mouse will fall beneath

your paws.

Your soft, swift paws

My innocent Bubastis?

Jacintha Buddicom, b. 1901
English writer

The playful kitten with its pretty little tigerish gambol is infinitely more amusing than half the people one is obliged to live with in the world.

Lady Sydney Morgan (1776–1859)
Irish writer

. . . a pretty playful kitten . . . is now pert and roguish, now timid and demure, according to its own sweet will.

ANNE BRONTË (1820–1849)
ENGLISH WRITER

Of all my friends, she is the wisest.

OSWALD BARRON (1868–1939)
ENGLISH WRITER AND GENEALOGIST

This is my Man. I am not afraid of him.

He is very strong for he eats a great deal; he is an Eater of All Things. What are you eating? Give me some!

He is not beautiful, for he has no fur. Not having enough saliva, he has to wash himself with water. He miaows in a harsh voice and a great deal more than he needs. Sometimes in his sleep he purrs.

Open the door for me!

I do not know why he has made himself Master; perhaps he has eaten something sublime.

He keeps my rooms clean for me.

In his paws he carries a sharp black claw and he scratches with it on white sheets of paper. That is the only game he plays. He sleeps at night instead of by day, he cannot see in the dark, he has no pleasures. He never thinks of blood, never dreams of hunting or fighting, he never sings songs of love.

KAREL ČAPEK (1890–1938)
CZECH JOURNALIST AND WRITER

WHAT KIND OF PHILOSOPHERS ARE WE

WHO KNOW ABSOLUTELY NOTHING

ABOUT THE ORIGIN AND DESTINY

OF CATS?

Henry David Thoreau (1817–1862)
American writer

Take great care, especially with kittens,
in giving instructions. Ask how the cat
will understand them.

PHILIP WOOD, B. 1921
ENGLISH ECONOMIST

For she, that will with

a kitten jest,

Should bear a kitten's joke.

WILLIAM COWPER (1731–1800)
ENGLISH POET

NOTHING IS MORE PLAYFUL THAN A

YOUNG CAT.

Thomas Fuller (1608–1661)
English clergyman

*I*t goes into lovely tiger attitudes
when it thinks I am looking.

SAKI [HECTOR HUGH MUNRO] (1870–1916)
ENGLISH WRITER

Whence hast thou, then, thou

witless Puss,

The magic power to charm us thus?

Is it that in thy glaring eye

And rapid movements we descry,

While we at ease, secure from ill,

The chimney-corner snugly fill,

A lion darting on the prey,

A tiger at his ruthless play?

Or is it that in thee we trace

With all thy varied wanton grace

An emblem viewed with kindred eye

Of tricksy restless infancy?

JOANNA BAILLIE (1762–1851)
SCOTTISH DRAMATIST AND POET

A kitten is the delight of a household. All day long a comedy is played by this incomparable actor.

MONSIEUR CHAMPFLEURY [JULES-FLEURY HUSSON] (1821–1882)
FRENCH WRITER

Do you see that kitten chasing so prettily her own tail?

If you could look with her eyes, you might see her surrounded with hundreds of

figures performing complex dramas, with tragic and comic issues, long

conversations, many characters, many ups and downs of fate.

RALPH WALDO EMERSON (1803–1882)
AMERICAN WRITER

HER PRETTIEST TRICK, USED MOSTLY
FOR COMPANY, WAS TO LIE ON HER
BACK UNDER A SOFA AND PULL HERSELF
ALONG BY HER PAWS, IN FAST SHARP
RUSHES, STOPPING TO TURN HER
ELEGANT LITTLE HEAD SIDEWAYS,
YELLOW EYES NARROWED, WAITING FOR
APPLAUSE. "OH BEAUTIFUL KITTEN!
DELICIOUS BEAST! PRETTY CAT!" THEN
ON SHE WENT FOR ANOTHER DISPLAY.

Doris Lessing, b. 1919
Persian-born English writer

*N*o experiment can be more beautiful than that of setting a kitten for the first time before a looking-glass.

REVEREND W. BINGLEY (1813–1879)
ENGLISH CLERIC

This is the time for you to decide
where you want your kitten to
sleep. If you let it sleep on your
bed the first night it will expect to
cuddle up to you for the next
eighteen years or so.

GRACE MCHATTIE
20TH-CENTURY BRITISH CAT EXPERT

WE ARE SOOTHED BY HER REPOSE; SHE IS UNFRETTED BY OUR RESTLESSNESS.

Agnes Repplier (1858–1950)
American writer and critic

Upon the mat she lies and leers

and on the tawny throat of her

Flutters the soft and silky fur

or ripples to her pointed ears.

Come forth, my lovely seneschal!

so somnolent so statuesque!

OSCAR WILDE (1854–1900)
IRISH WRITER

Thus you may crawl into the pigeonholes of desks, fall into the flour bin, tumble into waste-baskets, sprawl out of cardboard boxes, topple from chairs, climb up screen doors, get entangled in electric wire or balls of yarn, slip off the bed, skid on a polished floor, get yourself all wrapped up in paper or knock over a flower vase. You are not to worry if you break anything, or spill water, or get yourself covered with flour, ink or paint. They won't be able to be angry with you and you will soon learn which of your youthful pranks please them the most.

PAUL GALLICO (1897–1976)
AMERICAN WRITER

They tell me I am beautiful: they praise my silken hair,

My little feet that silently slip on from stair to stair;

They praise my pretty trustful face and innocent gray eye;

Fond hands caress me oftentimes. . . .

Charles Stuart Calverley (1831–1884)
English poet

New-born kittens are like blank slates.

GRACE McHATTIE
20TH-CENTURY BRITISH CAT EXPERT

*B*eing born and coming to life was for me like waking up after a long, delightfully deep and lazy sleep. There was no hurry about waking up . . . for the first few days I did not even open my eyes. And then for quite a few more I simply lay there, squeaking and purring with my tiny voice, and with a constant supply of delicious warm milk always laid on by my mother. Although I cannot remember her appearance, how well I remember that feeling of well-being, when I cuddled up beside her—I think we were in a large open drawer at the bottom of a bed or wardrobe—the warmth of her fur, the tenderness with which she licked us and groomed us and taught us to be clean. After I was about a fortnight old I became aware that the world was not entirely populated by cats.

A.N. WILSON, B. 1950
ENGLISH WRITER

FOR OFT MUSETH THE CAT AFTER

HER MOTHER.

English proverb

It is the cry that a cat makes only

for her kittens—a soft trilling

coo—a pure caress of tone.

LAFCADIO HEARN (1856–1904)
IRISH-GREEK WRITER

The young cat opens his pristine mouth
and asks for milk. Slowly, tenderly, he
meanders an approach—always with the
fullness of youth, with clear eyes, and
his tail waving in the air. He drinks in
celebration. His tongue, curled up like
a hook, barely touches the white pool
in the saucer. . . .

The little plate lisps out its last liquid.

Raising himself up on his paws, his

wide-open eyes distribute

his thanks.

CZESLAW BEDNARCZYK, B. 1912
POLISH-BORN BRITISH WRITER

I was only a kitten, and I was too frisky to know about time. But I grew faster than the rose-buds did.

FRANCES HODGSON BURNETT (1849–1924)
ENGLISH-BORN AMERICAN WRITER

GATHER KITTENS WHILE YOU MAY,

TIME BRINGS ONLY SORROW;

AND THE KITTENS OF TODAY

WILL BE OLD CATS TOMORROW.

Oliver Herford (1863–1935)
English-American poet and illustrator

*I*t is a very inconvenient habit of kittens (Alice had once made the remark) that whatever you say to them, they *always* purr.

LEWIS CARROLL [CHARLES DODGSON] (1832–1898)
ENGLISH WRITER

Oh—big human friend,
you think I am so far removed from your fears and
doubts
that I cannot understand your disappointments.
But, if you will look into my eyes as I am
beseeching you
to do now,
you will see the nakedness of my soul,
and find your own vulnerability reflected.
So please, in your lofty aspirations, don't overlook
the invisible gifts I bring you.
Today I watched the wind whirling the snowflakes
about in a chaotic dance of white radiance.
The flakes reminded me of your feathered dreams, and
my excited paws rushed up to your desk to share
the magical soundless dance with you;
hoping that through my throaty message you too
could experience the joy I have found . . .
just gaze into my eyes, be still—and I will purr
deep
within your soul; dry your tears with my warm fur.
And your spirit will run laughing with me through
the spangled sunbeams.
And your heart will be a dance of radiant
snowflakes.

STEPHANIE WILSON, B. 1956
ENGLISH WRITER

The big brave Angel cat, folding a
>*rainbow wing,*

Stretched out his gentle paw

From Cat Elysium's door:

I'll find, purred he,

A kitten—you were kind—

You must not grieve for me.

This one might do, this timid
>*little stray*

Terrestrial night to my celestial
>*day:*

It cannot take my place,

No other could do that,

But though you cannot bring
>*me back, you might retrace*

Remembrance in a kitten's
>*pansy-face.*

JACINTHA BUDDICOM, B. 1901
ENGLISH WRITER

ALL YOUR WONDROUS WEALTH OF

>HAIR . . .

DARK AND FAIR,

SILKEN-SHAGGY, SOFT AND BRIGHT

AS THE CLOUDS AND BEAMS OF NIGHT,

PAYS MY REVERENT HAND'S CARESS

BACK WITH FRIENDLIER

>GENTLENESS. . . .

Algernon Charles Swinburne (1837–1909)
English poet and critic

The kitten in the evening pursues

his shadow.

MADAME ADELE MICHELET (1826–1899)
FRENCH WRITER

THE MOON-COLOURED CAT

IS WALKING BY THE RIVER

HER FUR RIPPLES

LIKE RIPPLING WATER

THE MOON-COLOURED CAT

FLOWS GENTLY ALONG

BESIDE THE PURRING RIVER. . . .

Michael Bullock, b. 1918
English-born Canadian writer and scholar

ILLUSTRATION ACKNOWLEDGMENTS

COVER: *Kittens Playing*, Henriette Ronner

p. 2–3, 33: *All in a Row*, Agnes A. Talboys
(Fine Art Photographic Library Limited)

p. 7: (*Untitled*), Michael Langham Rowe (Wildlife Art Agency)

p. 8: (*Untitled*), Ernest Hyde

p. 10 [detail], 11: (*Untitled*), Ernest Hyde

p. 13: *Idle Moments*, Charles Edward Wilson
(Fine Art Photographic Library Limited)

p. 14: *Coaxing is Better than Teasing*, Charles Burton Barber
(Fine Art Photographic Library Limited)

p. 16: *Feline Fancy*, Victor Tadaro
(MacConnal-Mason Gallery, St. James's, London SW1)

p. 18 [detail], 19: (*Untitled*), Anne Briggs

p. 20: *Two Young Girls Playing with a Kitten*, Vittorio Tessari
(MacConnal-Mason Gallery, St. James's, London SW1)

p. 22: *The Little Anglers*, Horatio Henry Couldery
(Fine Art Photographic Library Limited)

p. 24: *Kittens at Play*, Henriette Ronner
(MacConnal-Mason Gallery, St. James's, London SW1)

p. 26: *Beauties and Toilet*, Horatio Henry Couldery

p. 28–29 [detail]: *Kittens*, Henriette Ronner
(Fine Art Photographic Library Limited)

p. 31: *A Little Upset*, Ada Elizabeth Tucker
(Fine Lines (Fine Art), Shipston on Stour, Warks)

p. 34: *Miss Ann White's Kitten*, George Stubbs
(Bridgeman Art Library Limited, London)

p. 36 [detail], 37: *The Proud Mother*, Henriette Ronner
(Fine Art Photographic Library Limited)

p. 39 [detail]: *The Intruder*, William Henry Hamilton Trood
(MacConnal-Mason Gallery, St. James's, London SW1)

p. 40: *An Armful of Mischief*, Catherine Caroline Cathinka
Amyot (MacConnal-Mason Gallery, St. James's, London SW1)

p. 43: *Woman with a Cat*, Auguste Renoir (Gift of Mr. and
Mrs. Benjamin E. Levy. Copyright © 1993 National Gallery of
Art, Washington)

p. 44: *The Fisherman's Daughter*, Charles Edward Wilson

p. 46–47 [detail]: *The Vantage Point*, Brenda Burke